THE COMPLETE GUIDE

GUINEA PIG CARE   DIY TOYS   POPCORNING   GUINEA PIG SUPPLIES

GUINEA PIGS

Advice from a kid

SICILIA TALIA

Copyright © 2020 by Sicilia Talia

All rights reserved.
This book or any portion thereof may not be reproduced or used in any manner whatsoever without the express written permission of the publisher except for the use of brief quotations in a book review or scholarly journal.

The information in this book is true and complete to the best of our knowledge. All recommendations are made without guarantee on the part of the author or publisher. The author and publisher disclaim any liability in connection with the use of this information.

Images reprinted under the Creative Commons Attribution 3.0 license

ISBN 978-0-9978605-3-5 (paperback)
ISBN 978-0-9978605-4-2 (ebook)

For any questions, please contact GuineaPigBook@gmail.com

November 2020
First Edition

Contents

Acknowledgement.................................... v
1. Introduction....................................... 1
2. Home Sweet Home 9
3. Munch Munch..................................... 21
4. Guinea Pig Breeds 29
5. Adopting a Guinea Pig - The Basics 37
6. Guinea Pig Health 43
7. Can a Guinea Pig use a Litter Box? 47
8. Guinea Pig Sounds 49
9. Funny things Guinea Pigs Do 51
10. Guinea Pig Myths 53
11. Dangerous Products 55
12. Make Fun Toys from Free Things 59
13. Pizza & Sushi 67
14. When I Got Guinea Pigs 71
15. My Experience Having Pet Guinea Pigs 73

Meet the Author..................................... 77

Acknowledgement

Thank you to my parents for your help and inspiration to write this book. Thank you to my mom for encouraging me and guiding me through the book publishing process. You encouraged me to pursue and follow my dreams. Thank you to my dad for teaching me to love learning and try my best in everything I do.

To all the pets in my life: Angel, Koshka, Melon, Zmeya, Dante, King Korcula, Francesca, Lincoln, Caterpillar, Sweet Pea, Chestnut, Milo, and my many fish.

Also Jackie, Trixie, Rambo, and Bandit.

1. Introduction

Have you ever thought about getting guinea pigs? Do you want to convince your parents that this is a good pet? This book will tell you everything you need to know about taking care of guinea pigs. You will learn about care, food and supplies, including time commitment. You will also learn about cool things guinea pigs do. I will teach you how to make DIY custom toys from things you find in the house. I will also share my experience with having piggies!

Pets are a big responsibility, including guinea pigs. Having piggies is very rewarding. It will teach you responsibility and will change your life forever! There are so many cool and funny behaviors that guinea pigs do!

Guinea pigs enjoy being outside!

Are guinea pigs the right pet for you?

Here are some key points to think about before trying to answer this question.

1. **Guinea pigs** require daily commitment and care. This means that you will have to dedicate at least 30 minutes of your day to care for your **guinea pigs**.

2. **Guinea pigs** are prey animals. They have a natural instinct to hide. It takes time for your guinea pig to get used to you and the environment they live in.

3. **Guinea pigs** require basic supplies. You need to have a cage, water bottle, food (hay and pellets), fleece or bedding, and hideys.

4. **Guinea pigs** are great pets. They are so unique and fun. They are so cute and easy to handle.

Personally, I recommend getting **guinea pigs**. I'm sure you will be a happy guinea pig owner!

What I learned in the first month!

When I first got my piggies, they were very scared. We brought them home in a carrier. Being in a car can be very scary for **guinea pigs** so I put some hay and food in the carrier. I also put some toys to make the experience less stressful. This is what I learned in the first month.

- **Poop Monsters:** **Guinea pigs** poop all the time! For such small animals, they poop a lot, so cleaning the cage is very important! I was really surprised because the poop doesn't smell and it's really easy to clean.

- **Hideys are important!** When my **guinea pigs** first went into their new home, they explored a little and went straight into the hideys. The first week they were very scared and spent a lot of time in their hideys, but after a week they started getting less scared and eventually came out more. Hideys are very important. All piggies need a hidey!

- **Eat your veggies!** One thing I learned is to say the same thing when you feed them their veggies. They will quickly learn the sound of your voice and will come every time you say the phrase!

Tips to help a scared piggie!

- **Be patient!** This is the number one rule to help a stressed guinea pig! If your piggie is really scared, it might take a while for them to get used to you. Some **guinea pigs** are not scared at all and some are.

- **Piggie Friends:** Make sure you have 2 or more guinea pigs. All guinea pigs need a companion. This will help them feel less scared in their new environment and will encourage them to explore more.

- **Provide hideys!** When your guinea pig first arrives at your home, they will be very scared. Make sure there's a hidey at all times! Guinea pigs are prey animals and hideys will make them feel safe. If your guinea pig is ever scared or stressed, a hidey will help them!

- **Feed them their favorite veggies.** Guinea pigs love veggies! Especially lettuce, cucumbers, and carrots. If your guinea pig is scared to be picked up or handled try hand feeding them. You can do this by putting a veggie in your hand and feeding it to them. This will help them know you're safe because you have food.

What are rodents?

You might wonder what a rodent is or why guinea pigs are classified as a rodent. Many people think that a rodent is any small animal. That is not always true. A rodent is a mammal whose teeth never stop growing. Guinea pigs have 20 teeth that never stop growing. This is why hay is very important in their diet. Hay will wear down their teeth and will prevent tooth problems. Some other rodents are rats, mice, hamsters, beavers, porcupines, capybaras and much more!

What are rodents? | 5

Guinea pig showing its teeth.

Guinea pigs are born with teeth that keep growing for the rest of their lives.

How to convince your parents to get a guinea pig

- **Make a poster or a presentation.** The presentation should show your research on care and time commitment. By doing this, you will demonstrate that you know how to take care of guinea pigs. This will show that you are responsible and you will be able to show off all the things you have researched and learned about guinea pigs. Also, this will prove you are willing to spend a lot of time taking care of your piggies!

- **Be ready for questions!** Your parents will ask a lot of questions, so you have to be ready. You can think of some frequently asked questions and find answers.

Some questions to think about

- How much space do guinea pigs need?
- What do guinea pigs eat?
- What is the average cost to take care of guinea pigs?
- Will you take care of them? How can you prove you will continue to take care of them?
- Do they smell?
- What supplies do you need?
- Will they get along with other pets? (If you already have other pets)

There are so many more questions so make sure you are ready!

- **Do your research!** This is probably the most important step. If you try to ask your parents to get guinea pigs without knowing anything about them, they will most likely say no.

There are so many places you can find out information. Here are some examples:

- **Read a book.** You can get a lot of information from reading a book, there are so many books that will help you. You already have this step done because you're reading this book!

- **Do research online.** There are so many ways you can find information online. You can read articles and watch videos. You can even search up questions that you may have. Just make sure you are getting your information from good reliable sources.

Know all the steps to taking care of **guinea pigs** such as setup, food, time commitment, and facts about them. Put them all in one place such as a presentation and prove you're responsible by showing you know how to care for **guinea pigs**.

You also need to know that a guinea pig is a lot of work and responsibility. You need to be able to commit time to take care of your guinea pig. The average lifespan for a guinea pig is 5-8 years. So you need to make sure you will still be able to take care of them and spend the time.

> Guinea pigs have an odd number of toes.

8 | INTRODUCTION

A guinea pig is a great pet and a wonderful companion.

Guinea pigs popcorn when they are happy or excited.

2. Home Sweet Home

What supplies you need.

- **A cage or enclosure.** You need this so your guinea pig won't escape. I found that the cages in most pet stores are way too small. The minimum amount of space needed for one guinea pig is 7.5 square feet. This is the minimum. A lot of the pet store cages are too expensive for the space given. The type of cage I recommend is a c&c cage. This cage was originally used as plastic shelves but can be used as a cage. The good thing about this is it is usually cheaper and you can set it up anyway you want. Also, I recommend using a metal wire cage instead of a glass cage because it is easier to clean and it helps your piggie get more fresh air.
- **Fleece or bedding.** You need fleece or bedding to put on the bottom of your cage. You can either use fleece or regular bedding.
    - **(Bedding)** If you are using bedding you can use cardboard or paper bedding found in most pet stores. This can get expensive because the bedding is not reusable and you will need to buy it over and over again. You can also use wood shavings as bedding but be careful

because certain types of wood is harmful to piggies. Do not use cedar or pine shavings because it is irritating to their skin and can cause respiratory issues and allergies. With bedding you need to spot clean everyday and replace bedding once a week.

- **(Fleece)** You can also use fleece. I recommend fleece because I think it is easier to use. You only need to buy fleece once so it is not too expensive. When using fleece, you need to spot clean it everyday (pick up poop, and hay) and wash it once a week.

- **Water bottle.** You need a water bottle so your piggie can drink water anytime they want. This is really easy to set up. You just attach it to the metal wire cage. You need to clean their water bottle and replace the water everyday. If you don't, algae will develop in the water bottle.

- **Hidey.** A hidey is very important. A hidey gives your guinea pig a place to hide if they're scared. They also sleep in their hidey. You will always need a hidey. There are so many different types of hideys such as wood hideys and fleece hideys. A second level in your enclosure, can double as a large hidey. You can buy a hidey in most pet stores and you can even make one yourself. My number one rule with hideys is one hidey per guinea pig. For example, 2 piggies, 2 hideys, 3 piggies, 3 hideys, and so on. This is really important so your **guinea pigs** don't fight over the same hidey.

Guinea pig sitting in its willow bridge hidey.

- **Food Bowl.** You need a food bowl to keep your guinea pig pellets or veggies in. Make sure you get a ceramic bowl or another type of heavy bowl so your piggies won't knock the bowl over. My piggies like to do that.

Guinea pigs can live up to 10 years.

Cute guinea pigs next to the food bowl.

- **Hay Rack.** A hay rack is not a must have but I would definitely recommend having one! You just hook this on your cage and put the hay inside. This helps keep the hay fresh and prevents your piggies from making a mess.

- **Chew Toys.** You need chew toys because guinea pigs teeth never stop growing. A lot of things made of wood can be a chew toy such as cardboard. Just make sure your piggie doesn't chew on anything made of plastic.

- **Playpen or Metal Gate.** You need this if you want to bring your piggies outside of the cage or if you want to bring them out for floortime.

- **Nail clipper and brush.** You will need a nail clipper to trim your guinea pig's nails. You will need to trim your piggies nails so they don't overgrow. Untrimmed nails can lead to many health problems. You don't always need a brush but it's a good idea to have one. If you have a piggie with long hair that requires a lot of maintenance you will need to brush their hair regularly.

- **Pet Carrier.** You need this to bring your guinea pig home. Also, you would need one if you need to bring your guinea pig to the vet.

Different types of cages/enclosures

- **Store bought cages:** Generally, store bought cages are usually too small. Store bought cages are too expensive for the space they are giving you. I recommend using a cage with more space. Most store bought cages are made with metal wire but you need to make sure the cage is at least 7.5 square feet.

- **C&C cage:** I recommend using a C&C cages. It is usually much cheaper than a store bought cage. The good thing about C&C cages is you can set it up anyway you want. It is very easy to set up and only takes a couple minutes.

- **Aquarium:** This is **not** recommended. Aquariums are usually very small. They are also very expensive. Since the cage is made of glass, it can get very hot. Your guinea pig won't get a lot of fresh air and it's more difficult to clean.

- **Wood cage:** You can build a wood cage yourself. This is probably the best option but can be hard if you never built anything with wood before. When building a wood cage it can usually be cheaper. Just make sure to use wood that is safe for guinea pigs. In addition, make sure there are no nails sticking out, or anything that may harm your piggie.

- **Outdoor hutch or shed:** If your piggies live outdoors, they will either live in a hutch or a shed. You can build one yourself and buy one. You need to remember that the shed/hutch should be fully inclosed so no predators can get in.

Guinea pig in its outdoor enclosure.

C&C Cage

Recommended space for enclosures

Number of Guinea pigs	Minimum Space	Recommended Space
One guinea pig (Not recommended, you always need more than one piggie)	7.5 square feet	8 square feet
Two guinea pigs	7.5 square feet	10.5 square feet
Three guinea pigs	10.5 square feet	13 square feet
Four guinea pigs	13 square feet	15 square feet

I recommend more space than the minimum requirements. The more space the better!

Fleece vs Bedding

	Pros	**Cons**
Fleece	• Cheaper (you only need to buy fleece once) • Reuseable (Better for the environment) • Personally I think it's easier to clean • A lot of fleece comes with a snuggle pocket, that is good for burrowing instincts. • Fleece is better for their feet.	• You have to wash it every week. • You need to spot clean more often.
Bedding	• You don't need to wash it, you just throw bedding away at the end of the week. • Don't always need to spot clean everyday. • Most pet stores sell bedding.	• A lot of beddings are bad for guinea pigs such as cedar or pine wood shavings. • Can be very expensive because you have to buy it over and over again. • Bedding can lead to many health problems if not properly cleaned. • Some guinea pigs are allergic to bedding

Keeping your guinea pigs outdoors

Many owners keep their guinea pig outdoors. Most owners keep their guinea pig indoors. If you want to keep your guinea pig outdoors here are some things to think about.

- Make sure the weather is not too cold or hot. If it gets too cold or too hot, you're going to have to take them inside. The ideal temperature is 65 to 75 degrees fahrenheit. If you're keeping your guinea pig indoors for the winter and outdoors for the summer it's good to bring them out in the spring. This will help them get used to the weather. Make sure the weather is not too cold.

- Other animals such as chipmunks and groundhogs can dig underneath and get into your cage. You need to put metal wiring or cement on the bottom of the cage so animals can't get in.

- If you are letting your **guinea pigs** eat the grass and plants in your yard you have to make sure there's no chemicals. Even if you don't put chemicals in your yard your neighbors may and this can possibly runoff into your yard.

- You will need a top for your cage. You need this because **guinea pigs** are prey animals. You will need to keep them safe from predators such as hawks.

- Having your guinea pigs live outside exposes them to mites, fleas, and other parasites. There are lots of insects outside and it's easier to get exposed to them outdoors than indoors.

*There are so many more things to research about having your piggies live outdoors. I recommend having your **guinea pigs** live indoors because I think it will be easier and you get to see them all the time.*

Indoor vs Outdoor

Where	Pros	Cons
Indoor	• No predators. • No need to worry about other animals attacking them. • You can see your guinea pigs all the time. • It is usually cheaper. • Temperature: • No need to worry about the temperature getting too hot or cold.	• Not a natural habitat for your guinea pigs. • They don't get to eat grass outside. • It can make the room smell bad. • You might have to clean the cage more. • Your guinea pig cage will take up space in your house.
Outdoor	• More of a natural environment. • They can eat the grass outdoors • No need to clean as often.	• Could be too hot or cold. • You might have to bring them inside for part of the year • You need to make sure your cage is fully enclosed so predators won't get in. • You don't see your guinea pigs as often.

I recommend having your guinea pig live indoors. My guinea pigs *live indoors. I think it's a lot more work for your piggies to live outdoors.*

I bring my guinea pigs *outdoors in the summer. I have a playpen that I put them in. I don't bring them out too often and I only bring them out a couple times in the summer or spring. They are usually only out for a couple hours with supervision.*

My daily cleaning routine

1. **Remove:** I take everything out of their cage (Hideys, food bowls, hay rack, litter box and toys).
2. **Sweep:** Then I get a dustpan and sweep up all the poop and hay.
3. **Throw Away:** I throw away the old hay in their litter box.
4. **Clean Hideys:** I clean their hideys and food bowl.
5. **Refill Water Bottle:** Clean their water bottle and put in new water.
6. **Refill Hay rack:** Put new hay in their hay rack.
7. **Add New Hay:** I put new hay in their litter box.
8. **Refill Pellets:** I give them about ¼ cup pellets in their bowl.
9. **Rearrange:** Put everything back into the cage. I like to rearrange their cage so they won't get bored and they will have new opportunities to explore.

I also wash the fleece once/twice a week.

> Guinea pigs have four toes in the front and three toes in the back.

What do you call a guinea pig with three eyes?

A guinea piiig.

3. Munch Munch

Basic Foods

Hay: Guinea pigs need fresh hay daily. Hay is very important to guinea pigs and should be about 80% of your guinea pig's diet. They need to have unlimited hay. Timothy hay is a good choice of grass hay as it is nutritious, high in fiber and easy to digest. I recommend feeding timothy hay and buying the hay in bulk from a local farm because it's usually cheaper and higher quality.

Pellets: Guinea pigs need about ⅛ cup of pellets daily. Only feed ⅛ cup pellets daily because over feeding pellets can lead to health problems. Don't buy pellets with dried fruits, seeds or oats. Make sure the pellets don't have any artificial flavors or colors. You don't need to feed pellets if you feed your piggies enough veggies. I recommend feeding pellets because most owners are unable to provide enough veggies for your piggies to eat.

Veggies: Feed 10% or more of their diet of veggies daily. You can feed more veggies depending on how much pellets you give them.

Fruits: *Feed once or twice a week.*

Feed raw leafy green veggies daily and give your piggie a variety of different veggies.

You can give **guinea pigs** the scraps of the veggies you don't eat.

What fruits and veggies can guinea pigs eat?

Veggies (all veggies must be raw)

- **Cucumbers:** Guinea pigs love cucumbers. Cucumbers don't have much sugar. Although they don't have much nutritional value; cucumbers can be fed a few times a week.
- **Kale:** Guinea pigs can eat kale daily or a few times a week. The kale stems are really good for the guinea pig's teeth.
- **Broccoli:** Broccoli is good to feed a few times a week.
- **Celery:** Celery can be fed to guinea pigs and it contains vitamin C.
- **Bell Peppers:** Guinea Pigs can eat bell peppers. Yellow and red bell peppers have the most vitamin C.
- **Parsley:** Parsley is very healthy for guinea pigs and can be fed three times a week.

WHAT FRUITS AND VEGGIES CAN GUINEA PIGS EAT? | 23

Guinea pig enjoying yummy carrots.

The oldest guinea pig lived for 14 years and 10 months.

Fruits

- **Apples:** Apples are safe to eat and don't usually cause any problems. Most guinea pigs love apples!
- **Bananas:** Bananas are high in sugar so should be fed as an occasional treat. Don't feed the piggies banana peels.
- **Pineapple:** Guinea pigs can eat pineapple. Only feed fresh pineapple. Do not feed dried or canned pineapple.
- **Mango:** Guinea pigs seem to really like mango! Mango should only be fed in small amounts once a week.
- **Oranges:** Oranges are a great source of vitamin C. They should only be fed once a week.
- **Pear:** Pears should only be fed in small amounts and once a week or every two weeks.
- **Strawberries:** Guinea pigs can eat strawberries as an occasional treat but I don't recommend feeding the leaves and stems.
- **Tomatoes:** Tomatoes are a great source of vitamin C. Do not feed unripe tomatoes, leaves or stems.
- **Watermelon:** Only feed them a small slice of watermelon once a week.

Abyssinian guinea pigs love pineapple.

Fruits should only be fed once or twice a week.

Remember that not all fruits/veggies are on this list.

Do Not Feed these Veggies!

Iceberg Lettuce: One of the most common mistakes new owners make is feeding their piggies iceberg lettuce. Iceberg lettuce should not be fed because it has hardly any nutrients.

Avocados: The skin is highly toxic and the inside is too high in sugar.

Cabbage: Any kind of cabbage is bad for piggies.

Onions and Garlic: Onions and garlic are toxic for guinea pigs to eat.

Potatoes: Potatoes are bad for piggies, especially if they are green or sprouted.

Mushrooms: Don't feed your piggies mushrooms. Sometimes this can be found in hay. If you find a mushroom in their hay be sure to take it out.

There are so many more poisonous fruits and veggies that are not on this list. Make sure you know the food you're giving them isn't poisonous.

Poisonous Foods

Meat: Any kind of meat including fish is poisonous to piggies. Guinea pigs are herbivores and can't eat meat. Guinea pigs can only eat plants.

Dairy: Guinea pigs can't have dairy (milk, cheese, butter, or eggs). A lot of stores sell yogurt drops and I would not recommend feeding your guinea pigs because they are not healthy for them.

Alcohol: Alcohol is extremely bad for guinea pigs. Never feed them alcohol and because it can lead to death.

Chocolate: Don't feed chocolate to your piggies.

Bread/Cookies: This isn't good for guinea pigs.

Coffee/Caffeine Products: Coffee should never be fed to guinea pigs along with any other products with caffeine.

Popcorn: Popcorn can get stuck in their throat. Popcorn should be avoided.

Candy: Candy should never be fed to guinea pigs.

Processed Foods: Don't feed any processed foods to your piggies.

Spicy Food: Guinea pigs can't have spicy food.

Beans: Don't feed beans to piggies.

Nuts/Seeds: Don't buy any guinea pig toys or items with nuts or seeds.

Other Pet Food: Don't feed guinea pigs other pet foods.

Guinea pigs *are vegetarians. They can only eat plants. They cannot eat meat or any animal products.*

Not all poisonous foods are on this list. So make sure you do research when introducing a new food

What I feed my guinea pigs daily

I feed my **guinea pigs** hay, pellets and veggies daily. First I replace the hay in their hay rack. I give them unlimited hay. Then I give them about ¼ cup of pellets. I give them a little more because I have two **guinea pigs** and they eat ⅛ cup pellets each. Then I feed them veggies in the morning and veggies in the evening. I usually feed them a variety of different veggies on different days. Some veggies I feed them are romaine lettuce, cucumbers, carrots, bell peppers, kale, radicchio and more. I give them fruit about once a week. I like to give them different fruits every week. Some fruits I feed them are apples, bananas, blueberries, and strawberries.

Chestnut eating a pumpkin!

28 | GUINEA PIG BREEDS

Guinea pigs eat their poop!

4. Guinea Pig Breeds

Common Breeds

American: This is the most common breed of **guinea pigs**. This is a good breed to get as a first time guinea pig owner. They have smooth short hair that doesn't require any maintenance.

American guinea pig.

Abyssinian: The Abyssinian has 6-8 swirls of hair. Although its fur looks a little messy, they don't require any maintenance. The abyssinian is known to be the friendliest guinea pig.

Abyssinian guinea pigs.

Peruvian: This guinea pig has very long hair. In fact it is the longest haired guinea pig. I do not recommend this breed for a first time guinea pig owner because you have to take care of their hair and that requires a lot of maintenance.

Perurvian guinea pigs.

Rare Breeds

White Crested: The white crested guinea pig has smooth short hair. On the top of its head there's a white circle of fur. The white crested is the rarest guinea pig breed.

White crested guinea pig.

FUN FACT

The white-crested guinea pig is the rarest type of guinea pig.

Teddy: The teddy has short hair. The hair stands up like a teddy bear.

Silkie: The silkie's fur is similar to the peruvian but their fur doesn't go in front of their face. This also isn't recommended for a first time guinea pig owner because its fur requires a lot of maintenance.

Silkie guinea pig.

Coronet: The coronet's fur is similar to the silkie's, but on the top of their head they have white fur, like the white crested. This also isn't recommended for a first time guinea pig owner because its fur requires a lot of maintenance.

Coronet guinea pig.

Texel: The texel is similar to the peruvian and the silkie. The texel has long curly fur. This is not recommended for first time guinea pig owners because its fur requires daily brushing.

Himalayan: The himalayan's fur looks similar to a siamese cat. When exposed to a lot of sunlight their points will begin to fade away. They also shouldn't be exposed to too much sunlight so keep their cage in the shade.

Himalayan guinea pig.

FUN FACT

Guinea pigs live in herds of usually 10 in the wild.

Rex: The rex guinea pig looks similar to the teddy. They require not as much grooming as the perurvian or the silkie but they do need brushing regularly.

Rex guinea pig.

Skinny Pig: The skinny pig is a hairless guinea pig with some hair on its feet, muzzles, and legs. They are not recommended for first time guinea pig owners because they need a lot of extra care.

Skinny pigs require extra care.

Baldwin: The baldwin looks very similar to the skinny pig. They are born with a full coat of fur, but they shed and any remaining hair only remains on their feet.

Baldwin guinea pig.

5. Adopting a Guinea Pig - The Basics

Where to adopt?

There are so many places you can get a guinea pig. Here are some below.

- Most pet shops have **guinea pigs**.
- You can go to an animal shelter and rescue an abandoned piggie.
- Go on a website that gives aways rescue piggies and adopt a piggie.
- Go on an online discussion group or guinea pig forum.
- Someone you know might be giving away **guinea pigs**.

I recommend adopting **guinea pigs** from a shelter instead of buying one at a pet store. This is because there are so many abandoned piggies that need a friendly home. I adopted my piggies from a shelter when they were 4 years old.

Chestnut and Milo!

Can guinea pigs live with other pets?

Guinea pigs should not live in the same enclosure with other pets. I do not recommend having other pets and your **guinea pigs** living in the same space. Here are some reasons:

- **Dogs or Cats:** **Guinea pigs** shouldn't live in the same space with dogs or cats. Do not leave your guinea pig alone with a dog or a cat. Dogs and cats are predators and might attack your guinea pig.

- **Rabbits:** Rabbits are similar to **guinea pigs** but shouldn't live in the same enclosure. This is because rabbits and **guinea pigs** eat some different foods. If they eat each other's foods, this can be unhealthy. They may also not get along.

- **Other small animals:** **Guinea pigs** cannot live in the same enclosure with other small animals. Pets such as hamsters and hedgehogs use a wheel. **Guinea pigs** can't use a wheel, it will hurt their back. Also they eat different foods.

Guinea pigs can live in the same household as other pets but they should be separated while inside the house.

Not all pets are on this list but your **guinea pigs** *should only live in the same enclosure with other* **guinea pigs** *and not any other pets.*

If you do have a dog or cat, you should get a top for your cage. This way your dog or cat won't be able to get into the cage.

Author's Experience

Your guinea pigs should only live in the same enclosure with other guinea pigs and not any other pets.

If you do have a dog or cat, you should get a top for your cage. This way your dog or cat won't be able to get into the cage. I have two cats and two guinea pigs. When I introduced my cats to my guinea pigs, the cats didn't seem to care. However, one of my cats tried to stick his paw into the cage a few times. I keep my guinea pigs and cats separated.

One or two?

You will need more than one guinea pig. **Guinea pigs** are very social animals and will always need a companion. In the wild, they live in herds of 10 or more **guinea pigs**. Since they are prey animals they get very scared if they are left alone. So you need at least 2 or more **guinea pigs**. They will be more social and they will explore more and be less scared if you get multiple piggies. No matter how much attention you give your guinea pig it will not replace another piggie. So getting multiple piggies is a must.

Best Piggie Pairs

There are many different pairs of guinea pigs.

Gender	Gender	Pairing
Male (Neutered)	Female	BEST
Female	Female	BEST
Male (unneutered)	Male (unneutered)	YES Unneutered males can fight. Two male siblings that grew up together will generally not fight as much
Male (unneutered)	Female	NO

Bringing your guinea pig home

Bringing your guinea pig home can be very stressful for them. Here are some tips to help.

- **Use a carrier.** Always use a carrier when bringing you guinea pig home. This will be much better for them. Many pet stores give you a cardboard box to bring them home. There are many problems with this.
    - You could drop your guinea pig. The cardboard could break and you could drop your guinea pig. This is also very stressful for your guinea pig.
    - The cardboard boxes are often very small and your guinea pig can't move around.

-
  - It is very dark and there are little holes for them to breath.
  - Lastly if they poop or pee, the whole cardboard box will smell and make a mess.

- Using a carrier will solve all of these problems. It's big enough for your guinea pig to move around, it won't break, a carrier is more open, so your guinea pig will be able to get air, and it will be fine if they poop and pee in it. Many people give away free pet carriers and many rescue centers also give them away for free. I recommend getting a cat carrier because it is usually cheaper and has more room.

- **Line the bottom of the carrier.** You should line the bottom of the carrier, so if they poop or pee it won't make a mess. You can line the carrier with pee pads, fleece, newspaper and anything else that is safe for piggies.

- **Provide hay inside the carrier.** This will help your guinea pig feel less scared. They will feel more safe if they have hay and food around them.

- **Feed them veggies in the carrier.** Feed them veggies when they are in their carrier. This will help them feel less scared and they will trust you more.

Why was the Guinea Pig upset with his job?

It didn't pay enough celery.

6. Guinea Pig Health

Trimming their nails

Why Trimming is important

Trimming your guinea pig's nails is very important. If you don't trim their nails, it can lead to many health problems. Trimming guinea pigs nails can seem difficult at first but it really isn't. The first time I trimmed their nails, I was really scared but it was not hard.

- When trimming their nails, remember not to trim the pink part of their nail. This will hurt them and it will bleed. If this happens don't worry, just get a towel and put it over their nail to stop the bleeding. This will hurt but it will go away.

Tips on trimming nails

- **Don't trim too far.** If your guinea pig's nails are darker and you can't see the pink part, you can get a flashlight and shine it onto their nails. Just make sure you don't shine it in their eyes.
- **The back nails.** To trim the back nails, you can pick your guinea pig up so their back feet are sticking out. This helps so your guinea pig won't move around.

- **Distract with food!** You can feed them their favorite veggies to make trimming their nails less stressful. You could also feed them veggies after so they know that after you finish trimming their nails they will get veggies!

- **Blanket method.** If your guinea pig doesn't like their nails trimmed, you can put a blanket on them, with their feet sticking out. This way they can't move around that much. Make sure not to put the blanket too tight.

- **Frequency.** I like to trim their nails about once a month. I check to see if I need to trim their nails.

WHEEKly Health Checks

- **Overall health:** Check your guinea pigs' behavior weekly. They should be active and moving around. If they are sleeping more, seem more tired, or don't have any energy, this could be a sign of health problems.

- **Nails:** Check if nails are trimmed. If your guinea pig's nails look long, it might be time to trim them.

- **Nose:** Check their nose to see if there is any mucus. Make sure their nose is clear and not clogged.

- **Mouth:** Check their mouth and teeth. Guinea Pigs can get many teeth health problems. You should check if their teeth are growing correctly.

- **Eyes:** Check your guinea pigs' eyes. Make sure they are not cloudy or have anything coming out of them.

- **Fur:** Check your guinea pigs' fur. If your guinea pig is losing fur this could be a sign of a health problem. Guinea pigs don't have fur behind their ears so that is normal.

- **Ears:** Check your guinea pigs' ears. They could have mites.

- **Feet:** Check their feet. Uncleaned cages, stepping on metal wire a lot, especially untrimmed nails, can lead to health problems in their feet.
- **Eating & Drinking:** Check to see if they are eating and drinking. If they stop eating, that is a sign of a health problem.
- **Poop & Pee:** Check if they are pooping and peeing regularly.

This might seem like a lot, but this can be done in minutes. You can even do this just by looking and observing your guinea pigs.

Milo in his strawberry hidey!

Guinea Pigs can't make their own vitamin C, so they get it from the food they eat.

7. Can a Guinea Pig use a Litter Box?

Yes! Your guinea pig can use a litter box. Guinea pig litter boxes and training are different from cats or rabbits. Read below to find out how to properly set up your litter box and how to litter train your piggie.

How to set up a litter box

1. **Fit:** Get a litter box or bin that both your **guinea pigs** can fit in. I recommend using a rabbit or cat litter box because guinea pig litter boxes are usually too small. Many places also sell litter boxes called kitchens.

2. **Lining:** Line the bottom on the litter box with newspaper or scrap paper.

3. **Hay:** Put hay into the litter box. You can either put hay in the litter box or put a hay rack close to the litter box. **Guinea pigs** like to poop where they eat so if there's food near the litter box they will most likely use it. You can also fill the litter box with bedding.

4. **Location:** Pick a place in their cage where they go to the bathroom a lot. If you put the litter box in that place they will already want to go there.

Litter box do's and don'ts

1. Do not use cat litter for the guinea pig's litter box. Cat litter can hurt their feet and is really bad for them if they eat it.

2. Do not force your guinea pig to use the litter box.

3. Do not use negative reinforcement. If your guinea pig doesn't use the litter box, it's okay. Every guinea pig is different and some take longer to get used to using a litter box.

4. Do not get a litter box with metal wire on the bottom. This is really bad for their feet and can cause bumblefoot.

Tips on litter training

1. Use positive reinforcement. This is good because your guinea pig will remember the litter box as a positive place.

2. Give them treats or veggies. Try to lure them into the litter box with their favorite foods. You can put veggies in their litter box so they want to go inside. If you see your guinea pig in the litter box, give them a treat or veggie.

3. Put the litter box in a darker place. **Guinea pigs** like privacy when they poop.

4. Make sure the bedding you use is different from the bedding used in the litter box. I recommend using fleece for their regular bedding, and hay bedding in their litter box.

5. Make sure your litter box is big enough for all your **guinea pigs** to fit inside.

6. Remember that most **guinea pigs** will never be fully trained to use the litter box.

8. Guinea Pig Sounds

Wheeking: Wheeking is the most common guinea pig sound. They wheek all the time. They wheek to each other. They wheek when they want food. They wheek a lot at humans when they want food. Guinea pigs will wheek when they hear the fridge open, hear footsteps, when it's time for food, or when they are just hungry. Guinea pigs love to talk and wheeking is their way of talking.

Rumble Strutting: This sounds like a very low vibrating sound. It is used to show dominance and to show who's the boss. It can also be used to stop fights. There are many different meanings when they rumble strutt. Guinea pigs will often shake their butt and move very slowly when making this sound.

Complaining/Whining: Guinea pigs make this sound when they are annoyed. For example, when another piggie steals their food, when another piggie is too close, or they just don't want to share their veggies.

Teeth Chattering: This sound is made when your guinea pig is unhappy or bothered by something. They could be unhappy with something you do, another guinea pig, or anything else they may find annoying.

Chutting: This sound is made if a guinea pig is talking to themselves. Your guinea pig makes this sound when they are relaxed and happy.

Purring: Most people would think this is a happy sound similar to how cats purr. This isn't all true. They can purr when they are happy or when they are not happy. They will sometimes purr when you pet their butt because they don't particularly enjoy that.

Chirping: Pet guinea pigs don't make this chirping sound often. Guinea pigs usually make this sound when they think they are in danger.

One Loud Squeak: Pet guinea pigs also don't make this sound very often. They will only make this sound when they are in pain. If you hear your guinea pig making this sound you should bring them to the vet immediately.

It's illegal to own one guinea pig in Switzerland.

9. Funny things Guinea Pigs Do

- **Popcorning:** Popcorning is one of the cutest things guinea pigs do! Popcorning is when a guinea pig leaps into the air and does a little jump. Guinea pigs popcorn differently and some do more than others. Guinea Pigs popcorn when they are happy or excited!

- **Eating their poop:** Guinea pigs eat their poop. It sounds gross but it is common for piggies to eat their poop. This is normal and if your guinea pig does this you don't need to worry.

- **Freeze!:** Guinea pig will sometimes randomly freeze and stare into space. This is because guinea pigs have better hearing than humans, so they may hear things that we can't.

- **Eyes Open:** Guinea Pigs sleep with their eyes open. This might seem really uncomfortable but for them it's fine. They do this because they are prey animals and they always need to be alert. If you see your piggie sleeping with its eyes closed, this means they really trust you and the environment they live in.

- **Marking Territory:** They do this by dragging their butt and it looks kind of funny. Guinea pigs do this to mark their territory. They might do this when they are in a new place, or after you just cleaned their cage.

- **Follow The Leader:** Guinea pigs do this when they are exploring a new place. This is when they follow each other in a line. It almost looks like their playing follow the leader!

Milo in his maze!

FUN FACT

Guinea pigs like to chat with each other.

10. Guinea Pig Myths

- **Guinea pigs are boring:** Many people think guinea pigs are boring and sleep all day. This is untrue. Guinea pigs are very fun and interesting pets that play and popcorn. However, in small cages, guinea pigs will have limited space to run around and will tend to sleep more or stay in their hideys.

- **You only need one guinea pig:** This is probably one of the most common myths about guinea pigs. You need 2 or more guinea pigs. A lot of places may tell you that you only need one but that is not true. Having two guinea pigs will encourage them to explore more and they will be so much happier with a companion.

- **All rodents are the same:** Many people think that all rodents are the same. Other rodents are similar but are different. Guinea pigs eat different food than other rodents and have many different behaviors.

- **Guinea Pigs Smell:** Guinea pigs themselves don't smell and are actually very clean creatures. If you clean their cage regularly and replace bedding/clean fleece, they will not smell a lot.

- **Guinea pigs don't like humans:** This isn't true. Guinea pigs are prey animals and will take time to get used to being picked up. At first, it will be scary for the guinea pigs to be picked up. They will have a natural instinct to run away. From their perspective, it feels like a bird or predator is picking them up and they are being captured. It will take time for them to get used to being handled.

- **Guinea pigs don't require any maintenance:** Many people think that guinea pigs are easy pets. I don't think taking care of guinea pigs is hard but it can be time-consuming. I spend at least 45 minutes of my day taking care of them. I have two cats and I think taking care of my guinea pigs is more time consuming than the cats.

- **Two male guinea pigs will always fight:** This is not always true. Male guinea pigs generally fight more than females but they don't always fight. I have two male guinea pigs and they don't fight. They are brothers and have been together their entire lives. If you have two male piggies who have been together their whole lives they will most likely not fight. If you introduce two males who didn't grow up together they may fight. If your piggies do fight you will have to separate them.

- **Guinea pigs are starter pets:** This is a really bad myth about guinea pigs. There is no such thing as a "starter pet". Guinea pigs are not starter pets. Guinea pigs take a lot of time to take care of properly. You will have to spend at least 30 minutes a day taking care of your piggies. Guinea pigs poop about 20 times a day and that's about 100 droplets per day.

11. Dangerous Products

- **No wheels or exercise balls!** Many small animals need a wheel, but guinea pigs cannot use a wheel or exercise balls. This is because it is really bad for their back.

- **No plastic hideys!** Many pet stores sell plastic hideys. Guinea pigs will chew the plastic and that is really bad for them. Also, if it gets too hot, the inside of the hidey can overheat or the plastic can melt. Wood or fleece hideys are much safer.

- **No salt licks!** Many guinea pig books and pet stores recommend using a salt lick. Salt licks can be very harmful to guinea pigs. If you are feeding a well-balanced diet to your piggies you don't need to feed them a salt lick.

- **No metal wire litter boxes!** A normal litter box or litter tray is fine but don't buy litter boxes with metal wire on the bottom. Walking on metal wire can cause health problems such as bumblefoot.

- **No leashes or harnesses!** This is extremely bad for guinea pigs. Constant pulling on a leash will hurt their backs. Your guinea pig can also easily escape. Putting on a collar or harness can be very traumatizing for them. In addition, if you come into contact with a dog on your walk, the guinea pig may get hurt. Do not use a leash to walk your guinea pigs.

- **No vitamin C drops!** Vitamin C drops are a liquid you put into their water bottle. Your guinea pig does need vitamin C but does not need vitamin C drops. This is because the vitamin C will dissolve after about 5 minutes of being exposed to sunlight. After that your guinea pig is not drinking any vitamin C and also a lot of guinea pigs won't drink their water anymore because they will not like the taste of it. Instead feed your guinea pigs veggies with natural vitamin C, such as bell peppers.

- **No yogurt treats!** Do not feed yogurt drops or treats to your guinea pig. Guinea pigs are not supposed to eat dairy. Eating dairy can cause health problems. I recommend giving them their favorite fruit or veggies instead.

- **No small cages!** Do not buy your guinea pig a small cage. The minimum amount of space needed for guinea pigs is 7.5 square feet. A small cage will cause your guinea pig to be more bored, sleep more, be less active and will be more likely to develop health problems. Small cages are often very expensive. I recommend buying a C&C cage. These are cheaper, easier to set up, and you can design the cage yourself and add more space. A bigger cage is easier to clean because everything is more spread out.

- **No Lone Guinea Pigs!** Do not have only one guinea pig. You need at least two guinea pigs. This is because guinea pigs are very social animals. They live in herds of around 10 guinea pigs. They feel more safe when there's other guinea pigs around. They will want to explore more and will be less scared with others around. If your guinea pigs fight, it doesn't mean that they should live alone. What you should do is divide your cage in half, so each guinea pig can have their own space without being totally alone.

- **No swimming/bathing guinea pigs:** Do not make your guinea pig swim in water. This is really unhealthy for them and can make their skin really dry. Do not bathe your guinea pig unless a vet tells you to. Guinea pigs are not meant to be in water.

Guinea pigs are not related to pigs.

Guinea pigs are not from Guinea.

12. Make Fun Toys from Free Things

Using stuff around your house is cheap and easy. Useful items are tubes from toilet paper rolls, paper towels and gift wrapping tubes.

Remember to ask your parents before you use scissors.

Toilet Paper Roll or Paper Towel Roll

Save all your toilet paper rolls! These can be used to make many fun toys for your **guinea pigs**.

Here's three things you can make

1 Toilet Paper Roll Hay Feeder

Step 1: Take an empty toilet paper roll.

Step 2: Stuff hay or veggies inside the toilet paper roll.

That's it! You have an excellent hay feeder your piggies will enjoy. Leave it inside their cage, and watch them fight over the hay. Don't be surprised if the piggies chew the toilet roll as well.

60 | MAKE FUN TOYS FROM FREE THINGS

2. Toilet Paper Roll - Diamond Hay Feeder -

Step 1: Take an empty toilet paper roll and cut diamond shaped holes.

Step 2: Stuff hay inside.

3. Heart Shape Hay Feeder

Step 1: Find a box from your kitchen. You can use a cereal box, a cracker box, or any cardboard box.

Step 2: Cut holes into the cardboard box. The holes can be heart shaped.

Step 3: Put hay inside of the box with hay sticking out.

Step 4: Now you have a hay feeder! Watch your piggies eat hay from their new hay feeder.

Heart shaped hay feeder your piggies will love

4. Cardboard Hidey

Step 1: Get an old cardboard box. For example, get a delivery box.

Step 2: Cut an entrance into the box. Make sure the entrance is big enough for your guinea pig to go through. I recommend putting two entrances so your **guinea pigs** won't fight.

Step 3: Give the hidey to your **guinea pigs**!

Make sure there's no tape or writing on the box because they like to chew on cardboard. A lot of **guinea pigs** like cardboard boxes more than expensive store bought hideys!

5. Cardboard Ball

Step 1: Get a paper towel roll or toilet paper roll.

Step 2: Cut rings into the toilet paper roll. (about 4 rings)

Step 3: Place rings together into a ball.

Step 4: Hide their favorite treat or veggie. This is good because it helps them not be bored.

6. Paper Towel Roll - Toy Fence

This is a neat fence to lure your piggies to jump over using food. Here's what you do

Step 1: Get three paper towel rolls.

Step 2: Roll #1 - Cut one hole from the bottom (at the height of the guinea pig's nose) The hole should be 1 inch.

Step 3: Roll #2 - Cut another hole from the bottom (at the height of the guinea pig's nose) The hole should be 1 inch.

Step 4: Roll #3 - This will be inserted into the Roll #1 and #2 (to form an H shape fence)

7. Oatmeal Box Tunnel

Step 1: Get a used oatmeal box. Make sure there's no oatmeal left in it.

Step 2: Take off the top and punch out the bottom.

That's it! Watch your piggies enjoy their new tunnel. Piggies love tunnels and they will have so much fun running through their new tunnel.

Chestnut and Milo in their oatmeal box tunnel!

8. Other guinea pig cardboard DIY ideas

Maze for piggies!

A castle for piggies!

Other Guinea Pig Cardboard DIY Ideas | 65

Guinea Pigs only sleep for short amounts of time (5 minutes)

Why was the guinea pig upset with the diamond?

There weren't enough carrots.

13. Pizza & Sushi

Make sure to ask your parents before using a knife.

How to make pizza for piggies!

- Cut a thin circle in an eggplant. (You can use another veggie that looks like pizza dough)
- Cut the circle of eggplant into a triangle.
- Use a tomato to make the pizza sauce. I blended a tomato and used that to make the tomato sauce.
- To make the cheese you can chop a white veggie in little pieces. I used the extra eggplant to make the cheese.

68 | Pizza & Sushi

How to make sushi for piggies!

- Cut a 1 inch slice of cucumber. Then cut out the inside of the cucumber. It will look like a ring.
- Chop up carrot and lettuce (or other veggies) and put them inside the cucumber.

How to Make Sushi for Piggies | 69

Chestnut and Milo eating cucumber sushi!

The longest guinea pig jump was 48 cm (18.89 in).

70 | When I Got Guinea Pigs

Guinea pigs can sleep with their eyes open.

14. When I Got Guinea Pigs

I wanted **guinea pigs** for a really long time. I really like small animals, and I wanted **guinea pigs**, ferrets or rabbits. I remember going to the pet store and they let me hold one of the **guinea pigs**. I knew that I really wanted a guinea pig, so I did a lot of research. I read a lot of books and did a lot of research online. I watched so many videos about **guinea pigs**. I found that it was very helpful to watch videos.

After I did a lot of research I finally got **guinea pigs**. I found my **guinea pigs** on a website that is for abandoned or rescued animals. My piggies are from a shelter. I didn't know anything about them except that they were four-year-old boys. They were probably abandoned by their owners and brought there.

My **guinea pigs** were very shy. I think that this is because they are older. It took longer for them to get used to me. I would feed the veggies daily and this really helped. Now they are less scared and come out every time we call them.

I am really happy to have **guinea pigs** and I don't think it is that hard to take care of them.

Both my **guinea pigs** are happy and happy to see me too. They love eating food and exploring new hideys.

Knock knock!
Who's there?
Lettuce.
Lettuce who?
Lettuce in, we want food!

15. My Experience Having Pet Guinea Pigs

When I first adopted my **guinea pigs**, they were very scared. It took them about one or two months to get used to me. Now, they are not scared. My **guinea pigs** don't like to be petted often but they let me pet their nose, chin, and sometimes the top of their head. One way for your **guinea pig** to get used to being petted is to feed them veggies. When they are eating, you can pet them. Your guinea pig will probably not mind because they are eating food. This will help them trust you because they will link getting petted with food.

I taught my **guinea pigs** to crawl on my lap. Sometimes their back claws can be sharp, so I put a small fleece on me. I fed them their favorite veggies like cucumber, lettuce or radicchio. They were very scared at first and they didn't want to crawl on my lap. Chestnut is less scared than Milo and he would go right onto my lap and eat veggies. Once Milo saw it was okay, he started doing it too.

At first, my piggies didn't wheek a lot. When I first got them, they were very scared and they would hardly come out of their hideys. If I wasn't in the room, they would come out to eat food but when I walked in they would hide. Now they never do that. They sleep a lot in the open and never run away when I walk in. Now they talk much more. They wheek when I feed them.

Meet my Piggies!

I have two **guinea pigs** named Chestnut and Milo! They are four-year-old boys. Chestnut has brown fur. Milo has grey fur with white fur around his neck, like a little scarf! They are both Abyssinian guinea pig mixes. Both my **guinea pigs** have unique personalities!

Chestnut, the little hogger

Chestnut is the smaller guinea pig but he still hogs all the food! His favorite food is lettuce but he is not very picky and will eat everything! His favorite kind of hidey is a cardboard hidey! He doesn't like it when I trim his claws and always moves. When he moves his head down he sometimes looks like a little buffalo! He is less scared then Milo and comes out more. Overall he is a little more active!

Milo, the scaredy piggie

Milo gets more scared, but he is still the one in charge! He always gets to pick what hidey he wants first! He eats a lot of hay and pellets but he lets Chestnut eat veggies first! He doesn't mind letting me trim his claws. His favorite food is cucumbers. He is a pickier eater, and won't eat some veggies. Milo popcorns more than Chestnut. He is cute when he popcorns!

Meet the Author

Sicilia is a kid who loves guinea pigs! She loves animals. When she grows up, she wants to be a veterinarian. Sicilia loves caring for her **guinea pigs** and wants to continue to own pet **guinea pigs** throughout her life.

Printed in Great Britain
by Amazon